UNDERSTAND YOUR LIFE

KIRN S CHOUGULE

Inspiration from my mother

and

In loving memory of my grandfather

Contents

CHAPTER ONE

Introduction

The reason to write this book is every day in my life, my friends, colleagues, and relatives always come up with questions to me. As I practice meditation, read a lot of philosophy on life, lessons, and biography. where I try to create a connection between the universe, destiny, karma, and life.

Also, people (My circle) gets their satisfactory answer through my philosophy and life lessons.

In the 21st century (Modern Era) our day-to-day life, we go through a lot in the form of greed, hate, love, anxiety, curiosity, depression, rejection, and unknown emotions.

We don't get the direction, path, or answers to our situation just because of our lack of knowledge.

While reading this book, you required a high intellectual level with your subconscious mind to relate it to your situation.

The 21st century is all about materialistic things like cars, big flats, money, sex, and brands where humans don't exist.

And human is made up of mind, soul, and body where human does not require above mention things. The requirement of a human is within himself.

While reading this book, you will understand how to live life, why with whom, purpose, goals, and many more who are confused in life.

q

CHAPTER TWO

Logic

When we live our life with a high priority on materialistic things, we can lose our natural human intelligence. Such types of people don't have a purpose to stay on this earth which is integrated with society, people, and the universe.

Such kinds of people can visit the places, where they can find themselves, explore human beings, and explore nature. To understand themselves, which can create clarity in their life to stay on this earth. Every human being initially in their life doesn't know the reason to stay on earth or their purpose in life. But the end of the human being should not be like that.

Utilizing our own life for the betterment or growth of human beings is the goal of every human being. Whether it can be through technology, science, or humanity.

Those who are lost in their life or world can just explore the nature and world. Also, they can try several options until they get satisfaction through it.

So, at the end of life, the soul of a person can be at a satisfactory level. When they can't do anything at 60, there will not be regrets and that will be regret-free life.

The only thing that is important in life is self-awareness. Which comes from the subconsciousness of the mind. For the subconscious mind, humans need to struggle a lot spiritually like meditation, the concentration which takes humans into super consciousness sometimes.

Our struggle experience always made us think about life and human to create a path for others, so struggling to understand life is very important in the initial phase.

During this phase of the struggle, human also needs to focus on nature. In the 21st century, humans are exploring technology and science but they are not considering nature. Then that can be the destruction of the human species.

Our subconsciousness is not illumined by us or by time. Those who reach it never return to this materialistic world.

One who can approach the highest subconsciousness is not required to return to the materialistic world. Because the material world reflects the spiritual world like the mirror in river water. The material world is just a shadow of spiritual (reality). In the shadow, there is no reality. In the desert, there is no water, but the mirage, suggests that thing of water. In the materialistic world, there is no water, there is no happiness, no satisfaction, and no purpose in life but the real water of actual happiness is in the purpose of life, the satisfaction of work (Dharma).

CHAPTER THREE

Purpose of Life

We come on this earth through a human medium, without skills, habits, purpose of life, and identity. Our family, our culture, and our circumstances build us through values and principles. We go to school, get a higher education, get a 9-5 job or do business, earn to survive or to increase the standard of life, get married, and repeat the cycle.

Is this our purpose in life? Did we come into this world to repeat the cycle? NO

Many people don't know why they are living in this world, why they go to school, why they are doing their job and why they are doing what they are doing so let's start with WHY.

We go to school, to learn the values of life which hide in lessons and are kept in the book only. We go to school to learn different aspects of life and the purpose of life and how we will spend the rest of life in this world with a clear Mission and Vision. But we end up with 90% or distinction in boards.

We don't know who are we? And take admission to the next level of life without knowing the purpose of life. We mistakenly choose our path or are misguided by the elder one. Then we blame others for misguidance or blame destiny or blame God. But never took the responsibility for any mistake.

We move to a higher level of life where we do jobs from 9-5 or local businesses to survive. No interest in the job but still we do to survive. That's not life or your purpose in life. Purpose of life means what moves you internally and which makes you better surroundings (Society). We are here to serve people, society, nation, and the world in many ways

Serving Society makes others live decent life happily whether it is beggars, poor, lower class, lower middle class, animal, or anyone.

But we mostly forget this in our daily routine of life. If we can't help others to create a decent life and live it, believe me, we will not be able to live a peaceful life. If you want to go ahead in life with the satisfaction of living life then help others to move ahead and have the nature of learning from children, unknown people, different cultures, and nature

Always try to find WHY everywhere whether it's nature, science, culture, natural calamities, education, job, business, and life. It will help you to go ahead for the longer term. We required self-realization to know the purpose of life and only 5% of people have that example Swami Vivekananda, Gautama Buddha, Chhatrapati Shivaji Maharaja, Nelson Mandela, Sudha Murthy, Dr. Babasaheb Ambedkar, and Martin Luther king.

It's all about designing your own life through questions. Always ask questions to yourself like what you believe? What do you want? Why do you want? Is it relevant to your dream or mission in life?

CHAPTER FOUR

Secrets of life

It starts with the living purpose of each entity living on this earth. In every stage of life, we suffer the result of our work or get the outcome and suffer the result, that's called a KARMA. Whatever goes around comes around so always be aware and conscious of what you are doing and what you are thinking. For example, if you are thinking for good cause for others, then good things happen to you. If you are thinking bad cause for others, then bad things will happen to you.

CHANGE is the rule of nature, but it doesn't mean it's false. The manifestation of the world is true and real but it's temporary. Whatever you do, that will be temporary whether that's even the result of your KARMA. Because TIME is also an important factor in nature. That's why we say, every dog has a day. Don't lose hope. Also don't even have an ego for your time, because the time changed.

In this world, humans are not meant to live life like dogs and cats, without any direction, purpose, or mission/ vision. They must be intelligent enough to realize the importance of human life and refuse to live an ordinary /mediocre life.

A human should realize the aim of his life. Any human can decide his mission & vision of his life or he also can realize it later because realizing the purpose of life sometimes takes time. That takes a lot of time because after exploring the world or humans or themselves, they got to know their purpose in life. Many people go to the Himalayas to find themselves; many people go for vipassana a meditation method for self-consciousness, there are several ways to find the purpose of life. Every person chooses which is feasible for them or what is possible for them. You might be heard some news like an IITian became a monk or became a farmer or a teacher in a rural area school. They might understand their purpose to be here, in this world.

But humans looking for something as a purpose in the life-like material world. The material world is temporary; it came into human life at a particular cost and just vanish after some time. Our life is not meant to be focused on materialist life because lifeless things can't drive anything; we must be concentrating our energy on life, not lifeless things.

Living entities cannot be created or destroyed, they are integral to humans, nature, and the universe. If we go deeper into the matter of considering modern science, we can see a living entity in-universe that living entity is the business of all people who are not only living in this world but also in this universe. So here living entity never born and never dies. We can see each living entity is being served to another living entity in different ways, by doing this the purpose of each living entity is fulfilled and they also enjoy it by doing this. For example, the mother serves her child, the husband serves to family, the animal serves his master, the politician serves the public, and the shopkeeper serves to public. In this way, we can see that each living entity is in service with another living entity.

There is no living entity exempted from giving service to other living entities.

So constantly giving service is an important entity for humans that we can consider his DHARMA.

Religion is nothing, but it's just faith. Hindus can change their religion to Muslim, Muslims can change their religion to Christian, and they are just changing their faith which does not affect the service towards other living entities. Performing your service to other living entities is DHARMA which can never change even after changing your religion or faith. Serving other living entities is the secret to happiness. An alone and single person cannot be happy for a longer time with materialistic life. Every person needs to fulfill their purpose of living here towards living entity, the satisfaction gets from the service, bring the happiness on the face which can be the longer duration.

CHAPTER FIVE

Attachment

Every person has a dream to become someone like a doctor, police, businessman, etc. but then when they are on the same path, which they dreamed about it, their achievement level change. Where they trapped themselves in the attachment of position.

If you want to live the purpose of your life, then you must detach yourself from your position. Working selflessly is more important to become extraordinary on this earth.

Extraordinary people never attach themselves to materialistic life or any position. They just do their work with their explored purpose in life. That's why in this world hardly people are there who create history for humanity or the world like Nelson Mandela, Chhatrapati Shivaji Maharaj, Mother Teresa, Gautam Buddha, etc.

If we are attached to the position, designation, or people, we will face constraints to achieve the purpose of life or to become extraordinary.

Now many people must be thinking, about how to become detached from materialistic life or attachment?

Che Guevara was a former Minister of Industries of Cuba. But before that he was a medical student and was exploring South America then he saw the two sides of

America where he witnessed poverty, hunger, and diseases.

That phase of his life was the beginning of new revolutionary life and he became among the extraordinary who works towards the society and world. He realizes the need to work toward people but that was the detachment from designation and materialistic life, and attachment to within himself.

If we are not attached to ourselves from within, then we cannot become detached from modes of material nature. Designation and attachment are due to lust and desire.

And whoever, at the end of life, quits his body remembering his work (Karma) alone at once. After ending life, everything goes as days increases like brain, skin, nails, etc but not his or her work which remains long-lasting in the universe.

CHAPTER SIX

Reading

From day to day life we read a lot of stuff from morning to evening like newspapers, magazines, etc. but those readings are done by those who are involved in materialist life.

If you wanted to go beyond materialistic life or wanted to live an extraordinary life then go for non-fiction, self-improvement, biographies, and autobiographies.

It takes years and years to dissolve in a character who lives for society with the purpose of life. There is discipline, and core values like integrity. A person who reads daily has power over those people who never read.

A reader who reads daily can understand the diversity, have open-minded thinking, several ideas, a wide perspective, and live thousands of lives. The character of a person is built by books he read, raise in his family, and lessons from his life experiences.

Reading helps us to explore self from within and detach from material life. If a person never reads become, he doesn't have the clarity to understand the universe, diversity, and people. And until and unless he explored himself, cannot become extraordinary or cannot attain satisfaction from life.

At the end of life, he will only criticize himself and will have regrets for not taking efforts to his satisfaction

We must always engage our minds in reading this literature which helps us to enhance our growth and purpose in life.

The modern man of the 21st century struggles hard to reach Mars and the moon but he has not tried very hard to explore himself from within. This is a not difficult process. One must learn it from an experienced person who is already in practice. This can free you from all kinds of anxieties in life. One will be freed from all fears in this life. But achieving all this phase, Human beings have a lot of questions about themselves only which made them think about life, people, family, the world, and loved ones.

Because sometimes life situations are mixed with materialistic life and materialistic life.

In the next chapter, we going to discuss the same

CHAPTER SEVEN

Destruction

Sometimes in life, we stand in such a phase, that made us shiver from inside, goosebump comes, you can't think, your mouth becomes dry, you wanted to cry, your heart becomes heavy, and you can't stand on the earth.

Excessive attachment to materialistic things puts the man in such a situation. Such fearfulness and loss of equilibrium take place in a person who is affected by the material condition. When a man sees only frustration in life, he asks a question himself only, "why I am here?" because everyone is interested in themselves only and their welfare. No one is interested in supreme within the self. Conditioned of soul forget this and worked in materialistic life which made them frustrated after some time.

In materialistic happiness, we forget our purpose of life (KARMA) or our duty as an engineer, doctor, governor, Architect, labor, or businessman, to be performed towards society.

Behind materialistic life, we forget the moral codes of our duty. As human beings, we always have to fight for our moral duties towards society. Then whatever it takes, we have done to perform those duties. Like kings cannot engage themselves in any other occupation. If the king's kingdom lies in fighting with his cousins and brothers and reclaiming the kingdom inherited from his father, which he does not like to do. Therefore he will be considered fit to go to the forest which can frustrate him.

CHAPTER EIGHT

The past

We lived our lives, and give our best but sometimes some incidents made us think about the person, situation, or ourselves.

We loved a lot a person who is very important to us but that was the past still, the past never leaves us because that is settled down in our memories. we forgive, but never forget.

We are humans who have brains, minds, and memory that make us very strong mammals on earth as well as the weakest also. Because we have memory.

We spend those lovely moment's in trust with a person whose DNA is completely different from us but destiny wants something different that is the universe wants to create you the strongest person on the earth by giving you the most painful thing in the world.

That's a very deep wound on the heart which is very painful but great thing is that nobody can see that pain. But don't lose the hopes

Every goal needs a time frame, otherwise, there is no clarity to it. So always go with a time frame for each activity whether it's career or love.

Life will show you the worst part of it when there is nobody with you because that's the best opportunity for you to understand yourself.

Living alone with detachment is the guru mantra for life. But that's the most difficult thing in life as a human, we raise with emotions, love, attachment, and feelings. Overcoming those things is the biggest challenge. If we overcome the above feelings then we are on the nirvana path.

You have to understand that past will never leave you alone. You have to take your past with you in the form of memory, feelings, emotions, and most important lessons.

Past will irritate you, will disturb you, might be you had great memories but those are part of your past, those are pages of your book.

Might be your destination is away from you but the path will create by those past lessons. Past will make you stronger or weaker, that depends on you.

CHAPTER NINE

Challenges

In day-to-day life, we face a lot of challenges. It can be in personal life, professional life, or social life. Many times we convert challenges to the problem and go into frustration. Did you think at any point why challenges come in our life? If not then here you go.

Life is like building, where you can go up step by step. Until and unless you take the first step, you can't take the second step. Same here until and unless you face-first your challenge, you can't face the second challenge in life to go ahead. That's why many people are stagnant in their life in all circumstances.

When the challenge comes and you are not able to think, that's ok. Because problems can't be solved in the same state of mind. Take your own time to calm your mind. You can practice meditation for 20 minutes by inhaling and exhaling breaths on the ground. Don't overthink and think between the meditation. Detach yourself from situations or outcomes. Calming your mind can also take 2-3 days or more. You can practice different methods too like gratitude, yoga, and pranayama....

Then ask the questions yourself, why did you start this? Will this help me to accomplish my dream? Is this gonna affect to my mission and vision of life? Are these my core values?

And when you find the answers relevant to going ahead with a challenge then think about strategies for risk and mitigation so it will give you the confidence to go ahead in life to face the challenge. And convert that challenge to opportunity. This can apply to each level of difficulty.

Everyone can overcome challenges and convert that to opportunities but most of the time we don't know ourselves, so we lose focus on ourselves and focus on outcomes that made us overthink. Believe in yourself to fulfill your dream and face the challenge.

CHAPTER TEN

Search

In the last article, we get to know the purpose of the life concept to love a meaningful life on earth. After publishing the article I got no applause and positive responses from people and also questions related to the purpose of life. How to get to know our purpose in life? How do have self-realization?

To know your purpose in life, you have to first understand yourself to know your core values because I have seen business moguls achieve their ultimate goals, but still live in worry, frustration, depression, and, anxiety. What exactly prevents you from being happy? Again came core values and beliefs. The answer is they focused only on achievement and not fulfillment.

Being extraordinary does not mean to be extraordinary joy, happiness, love, and a sense of the meaning of life. These two skill sets feed off each other and make me believe that success without fulfillment is a failure.

You have to dig deeper and deeper to find your core motivation and core values, to activate your superpower and your WHY power. To access point to your WHY power is through your core values, which defined who you are and what you are. Your core values are your internal compass, your guiding beacon, and your GPS. Getting your core values defined and properly calibrated is one of the most important steps in redirecting your life toward your grandest vision.

Defining your core values also helps make life simpler and more efficient. Decision-making also becomes simpler when you are in a certain difficult situation or worst turning point of life. Whenever you come to a difficult time of your life to make a choice, ask yourself, "Does this align with my core values?"

Enemies give us reason to stand tall with courage. Having to fight challenges your skills, and your character. A challenge forces you to assess and exercise your talent and abilities. Without motivation we can lose the fight and become lazy and fat; we lose our strength and purpose in life

In life, if we are not making the progress that we would like to make and are capable of making it; then it is simply that our goals are not clearly defined. Top-level people always have clear goals. They know who are they and they know what they want. Whatever they want, they write it down and they make the plans weekly, monthly, quarterly, and, yearly for accomplishment. Unsuccessful people have their plans in their heads like fogs, which disappeared anytime and we say a goal that is not written is merely a fantasy.

CHAPTER ELEVEN

Facing the truth

Any person in his world who knows his purpose in life always has to perform through action to achieve it whenever a needy person asked for him. Then whatever efforts it could take to achieve it.

Sometimes, a situation made us act against our purpose or core values. And perform some other actions due to hard situations in life. But that's the only challenge for humans, what we choose. There is nothing like right and wrong. It all is depending on the situation with principles and morals.

If the head of the family is not able to follow his purpose in life, then it seems difficult to be performed by another member of the family or society.

If people are aware of their purpose, then it indirectly brings peace, happiness, satisfaction, prosperity, and spiritual progress in life.

Our Indian ancients already designed the lifestyle of a human being should be, like how he should live, and what rituals need to perform to achieve the purpose.

But most of the time, the elder person of a family dies and the rest of things get vanish with him as younger members of the family don't know.

Such kind of people are raised as irresponsible and brings the chaos to society and consequently, they forget the aim of life (Purpose of Life)

And people who don't have any guidance for life, are wasting the natural resources of the earth. Always give your vibrant presence to others, so they can get motivation and also inspire others too. Experience human is responsible to lead youngsters and youngsters also have a responsibility towards elders to gain knowledge from experienced people and avoid mistakes in real life. But when the world is full of the fullish population (who don't know how to lead a life for a better world) can destroy the humanity and world. When a human start working toward humanity or any real-life problem, he is living his purpose of life in the world for a better world.

CHAPTER TWELVE

Self-Realization without attachment

Any human in this world wants to become famous just by doing his work, then he needs to understand the absolute truth of life. The human who knows the absolute truth of life is not bound by any materialistic conceptions. Sometimes we are afraid to do some karma even after it is bounded to do for the betterment of the world. Those people have magnanimous attitudes toward others which becomes weakness of life and heart. When we start our life living without attachment, it is very difficult for others to take charge of our minds or influence us according to their emotion or thoughts, or deeds they want us to do for them.

Self-realization is a very high-aligned thing that a person gets after a lot of pain, meditation, and yoga. Because sometimes people don't get self-realization even after their spending whole life.

To get a self-realization number of activities are like spending their life for a purpose, for people, for society, or only dedicated to yourself (Mind, Body, Soul).

Self-Intimacy

you must be in question of what is self-intimacy, if we google it, we get this above definition, "According to Melissa Orlov, author of The ADHD Effect on Marriage, 'self-intimacy is about being aware of your feelings, caring about those feelings, and sharing them with your partner."

as you can see the above, the cup is broken but it doesn't mean that it's a waste or useless. We can create more beautiful before it was.

Same as a broken cup, the human heart is the same. It becomes more beautiful when it breaks. In life love never breaks, heartbreaks means, demand breaks, expectations breaks, deal breaks, desire breaks, hopes break, and trust breaks.

Life is like flowing water (Behati hawasa tha wo), which means go with the flow or become like water. Whatever we put in flowing water, it takes with them. so take whatever you can take in life, whether it's good or bad. Everything entity is important in life to understand the importance of life, people, universe, nature, or society. If you become life water, nobody can break you. If you become stiff or brittle, anybody can break you. Our daily life is all about events and we are surrounded by happenings. so don't give too much attention to people and the environment and don't react. In life, many times unintentionally people got hurt or might be you get hurt unintentionally. This does not call maturity or mature person. we have to live this life with, no enemies. so whenever you meet your ex or any friend, meet him as nothing happened. Because I consider we have a very small life.

Self-intimacy means we are not trying to convince others rather than being ourselves and relaxing. Also not trying to express too much whether it's love, anxiety, hate, or excitement.

We are not exceptional from nature, we are part of nature. so if we observe nature, we will get answers to our confusion and question like from egg to butterfly

Change

change is the rule of nature

Nothing is permanent

Each deed needs to be a balance

Energy can only be transferred from one form to another form

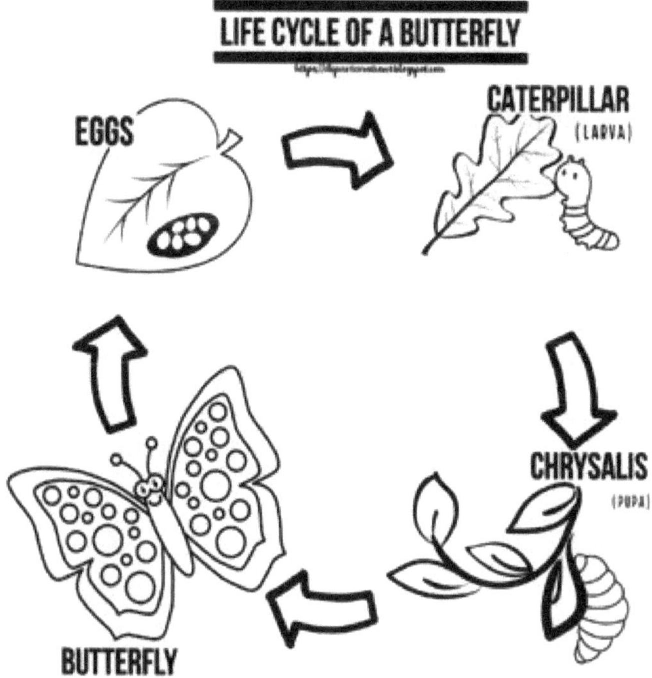

human beings with personalities are not stiff or stagnant. Every human being or person changes with time. it can be parents, cousins, friends, or colleagues, and that's the rule of nature. if you have good vibes or good karma, then destiny will make you help in any situation somehow or in any other medium. Even the person who is helping you committed bad karma or bad deeds. Nobody has a fixed personality, everyone changed. If you don't change, we will not be able to grow to fit in this nature or universe to survive.

we get hurt very easily by anyone's act but actually, nobody can hurt, you only hurt yourself. we are the only reason for our happiness or sadness or any emotion and that's self-intimacy. Expectations can destroy your self-intimacy, so it's better don't expect.

CHAPTER THIRTEEN

Practicals to do

In our daily life, we already were doing these things, to deal with people in the world or also deal with ourselves

1. Try to understand the person, understand the situation, and try to sort it out mutually and peacefully.
2. If 1st step doesn't help you, allow to happen and go with the flow. and be prepared for even unexpected situations.
3. Even if 2nd step doesn't help you, or they are at loggerhead with you then better communicate with them. all problems are arise from a lack of communication. If you both decide to talk then talk with love, calm, and peace. even if that doesn't work out then ignore them with love and don't react. consider them as immature and leave them in their situation. Might be they realize their mistake later and better. we can't force any human to realize anything because they closed the doors of it in mind. so never create any differences for such a person, sometimes it comes subconsciously.
4. Even after doing this activity, they don't turn out and then take a stick. this should be your final act. as our parents used to do it. only 90's children will be able to understand the fear of sticks. If that person is that

insensitive to understand differences, kya hi Kar loge tum? better to take the stick and make them understand better with that.

The above method was explained to deal with people but what about our inside where we most of the time disturb and hardly communicate. followed the same step even for the inner life,

1. Become stagnant in mind, means no reaction or emotion in mind. it should be calm even in the worst situation. meditation or yoga can help in this to maintain the mind's calm and peace. but the stagnant position of mind becomes very difficult for people who have never practiced meditation.
2. Give up on the situation and let happen what's happening for some while in your mind. whatever comes into your mind, will come for a while and go, that can be guilt, ego, excitement, or anything........ give up all those things. When you give up, you must be experienced freedom like in real life too... your problem is not the world, parents, friends, money, or loved ones. your problem is your mind. how you controlled your mind that defines you and your life
3. your third step should be your communication with your mind which can be done with the help of meditation, connecting to your inner body, soul, and mind, or some breathing techniques so it will be better communication with your better version. we get to know about ourselves if we are heading wrong. if you are clear inside, you are better clear outside. you bring more positivity, relaxation, and freedom inside. Negative actions create complexity and no clarity.

4. Even after doing this, we don't get what exactly we are looking for or have no clarity. Then here we cant take a stick and make understood what life is, that's why life gives you lessons, its called "life lessons" in terms of pain, heartbreaks, relatives, and society.

CHAPTER FOURTEEN

Trust, belief, and desire

Well, these words are known to everyone but not the exact meaning. If we understood the meaning, we would be applying it in life to achieve our dreams.

we lack to understand above mention keywords. so because of our lack of knowledge, we start to doubt ourselves whether we will be able to achieve our dream or not? or we start talking ourselves with statements like, this is not for me, I should go slow, this is the not right time, I am not the right person, I haven't done it before. This statement comes when you don't know your ability and you doubt yourself. If you would aware of your ability? you would be working on them, not doubtful on them. mostly people do not know their abilities so they doubt their abilities.

Even after knowing our abilities, we sometimes doubt our method or path and whether we are adopting the right technique or wrong. we doubt each term and path, world, people, and mentor.

Then doubting your achievement, doubting your life lessons.

these all doubts can harm our progress or any work, then our thinking comes into our action and then we surrender to our lack of knowledge.

CHAPTER FIFTEEN

Judging

people normally judge others from their perspective that's their consciousness, from their state of awareness and life lessons. The true self, judge themself first before judging others to understand themself first. When a person sees idiots everywhere it means he is the idiot same with the egoistic thing. If a person is egoistic then he will see another egoistic person, a second egoistic, and many more. It means that from nature he is egoistic, there is nothing to do with another human being.

Mind

we mostly listen to heart, but those who are diplomatic and practical, always listen to their mind, they observe their mind, and listen to what's in it. Whether it's love or hate or anger? so be always aware of your mind, for that observes the moments.

Your mind will tell you the harsh truth about life, which we are hardly able to listen to or believe. We humans can communicate through eyes, that's also in silence. what is takes to do that? it is our mind. the waves are there, the radio is also there, we have to only switch ON the radio and throw the electromagnetic field for a good connection. it is required not only for electronic gadgets but also for humans through the mind.

you only have to switch on the frequencies to get the things done or communicate.

sometimes we have low strength frequency so not able to connect with it. That required time so with time it will become strong if you required it (Desire).

So always focus on your mind, that's what you put in it or what mostly think or through about. whatever you have in your mind, you gonna put it in your life through actions. so be careful what you think, though, or focus on your mind.

In daily life, what you are focusing on that matters, distraction will be there to distract you from your goal or even if you giving reactions or feedback to other's opinions then you will be creating distance to achieve your dream or goal in a particular time which you defined. so it's always better to ignore the world and do what you have already set. because for world "change" is difficult to adapt or accept but for extraordinary people or mature people, "change" is very easy or even if not they never react to it negatively. they understand that change must be done with time.

You must also have questions like, what's going to happen, how, and what will be the destiny?

Well, you make no difference in this world, what's going to happen that's will happen. we can only take precaution and prevention steps. About destiny, when things happen according to your thoughts that will come to you.

Life is not fair and thats the life because life is all about happy, sad, anxiety, depression, adventure and many more. The more simpler the movies, the more boring it will be. So life will be difficult in some phases but your strength also greater than before and you will be enjoying life at higher level than before. so it will be worth it.

how you keep your attitude in your bad phase or good phase thats define you and your core values

Extraordinary

when a crazy human about his dream and passion wants to follow his passion or dream like hell. World call him idiot, mad or crazy until and unless he achive extraordinary phase or fame like non.

but in that phase, we face a lot of thinks, we thinks a lot about people, about dream whether we will achieve or not, if not then what people will think. but in all this things...dont forget that if you discontinue what you were doing, then world will be true one day for what they were saying about you.

CHAPTER SIXTEEN

Conclusion

After knowing yourself, you also get to know that, everything will change but there is something in you that will not change. And stick to that point in life to understand whether you changed, moved, or are stagnant. Always be relaxed, free, and happy because they can't be in tension and worry. Don't worry about what you gain and lose. Because who gained, they haven't done anything great with themselves. There is nothing to lose or gain.

When you experienced your life, and understand that we have to come out of a particular type of pattern and change ourselves first, rather than changing the world or others. That will be your freedom and higher achievement in life.

Printed by Libri Plureos GmbH in Hamburg,
Germany